D0521058

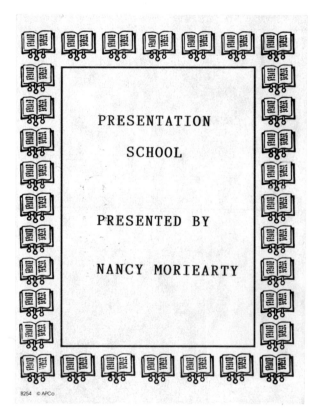

PRESENTATION

SCHOOL

PRESENTED BY

NANCY MORIEARTY

B254 © APCo

To the memory of Reg Birch—BB

First edition for the United States
published by Barron's Educational Series, Inc., 1996.

First published in Great Britain in 1995 by
Gollancz Children's Paperbacks;
A Division of the Cassell Group
Wellington House
125 Strand
London WC2R 0BB

Produced by Mathew Price Ltd.
The Old Glove Factory
Bristol Road
Sherborne
Dorset DT9 4HP

All inquiries should be addressed to:
Barron's Educational Series, Inc.
250 Wireless Boulevard
Hauppauge, New York 11788

Library of Congress Catalog Card No. 96-83309

ISBN 0-8120-6621-9 (hardcover)
      0-8120-9791-2 (paperback)

Printed in Hong Kong
987654321

MARIE CURIE'S
SEARCH FOR RADIUM

Beverley Birch
Illustrated by Christian Birmingham

BARRON'S

The room was like a cave gleaming with treasures.

Marie and Pierre Curie stood quietly together, looking. In the darkness around them, shelves and tables held the tiny glass dishes and bottles, glowing with a blue light, softly beautiful.

Like jewels on a dark cloth.

In that moment all tiredness, all years of struggle, all disappointments and accidents were forgotten. It was a moment of shared, silent peace.

On that icy night in the winter of 1902, in a ramshackle old shed in Paris, Marie and Pierre saw only the glow of the treasure they had brought out of the rocks and pine needles and brown crumbling soils of a distant land.

It was like reaching the peak of a mountain Marie Curie had been climbing for years.

She thought back to the years in Poland, as a young girl. Everything had been so hard! Teaching herself science with no teacher to guide her—just books, and more books, and her own fierce determination, and her dream that one day she would be free to study with other young people, in a university.

And always the battle to earn enough money to go to France. In Poland, girls were not able to study at the university. The university of Paris, in France, was the peak of her dream. Six years—working, learning, saving, working, saving, learning . . . and dreaming. And then on, to a new struggle in Paris, to master French so she could understand her teachers.

Listening, thinking, reading—six more years.

And all that had been four years ago, before her long, painful climb up the mountain had begun. That started the day she read about the invisible rays.

She had thought X-rays were strange enough. Rays of light that you couldn't see, that went through paper, wood, metal, and—most fascinating of all—the human body, so you could take a picture of a person's bones!

A German scientist, Wilhelm Roentgen, had discovered them only two years before, and now scientists everywhere were rushing to find out about them.

That's how a French scientist named Henri Becquerel had stumbled on another, different kind of ray.

A white metal called uranium, locked in a drawer, had sent out rays so powerful that they traveled right through a metal sheet and black paper. The rays had darkened a photographic film in the exact shadowy shape of the uranium.

Powerful rays, completely invisible, that no one had ever found before!

Madame Curie was aflame with questions: What were these rays? Did other substances send them out—not just uranium? What made them happen? How strong were they?

Becquerel found that they made electricity flow through the air.

She pondered the problem.

Perhaps she could measure how strong they were by measuring the electricity they caused in the air? Her husband, Dr. Pierre Curie, had invented just the machine—his electrometer. It could measure even the tiniest flow of electricity!

Eagerly she told him her idea.

Dr. Curie helped her arrange the machine. When there was nothing between its two brass plates, no electricity flowed in the air, and the pointer on the scale did not move.

But if something between the plates did electrify the air, the pointer *did* move. A little movement showed a small flow of electricity; a further movement showed a bigger flow; a large movement showed a very strong flow.

Madame Curie took her first step up the mountain.

Quickly she collected samples of all the substances used in the school laboratories where she and Dr. Curie worked. One at a time, she put them between the electrometer's plates and watched the scale. She tried lumps. She pounded samples to powder. She mixed, heated, cooled, wet, and dried them. Each time she wrote down what she put between the plates—if the pointer moved, how far.

Suddenly she could see a pattern. It didn't matter what she did to a substance—wet, dry, hot, or cold. If there was uranium in it, the pointer always moved. No uranium, no movement. And just as clear—more uranium gave stronger rays; less uranium, weaker rays!

She mulled over in her mind all she knew about uranium. It is what scientists call an element, one of the basic materials (such as gold, silver, iron, carbon, oxygen, and hydrogen), which make up all substances in the world. A new question was nagging at her. Did other elements besides uranium also send out Becquerel rays?

She took another step up the mountain. One by one she tested all the elements. One by one she found the answer was "No." That is, until she came to a gray metal called thorium. The pointer jumped high up the scale!

Her mind whirled. A hundred new questions: What about natural rocks, sand, soil? She expressed her thoughts to her husband. Out came their bicycles and off they pedaled on a new exploration.

Madame Curie's room began to look like a museum. Rock and stone—rough, smooth, hard, soft; purples and pinks and greens and shining black; grains of powdery sand, gritty dirt.

If she was right about the elements, then she should find that only rocks, soils, or sands that had uranium or thorium in them would send out the rays. Rock after rock, soil after soil went between the electrometer's brass plates.

Every single sample without thorium or uranium showed no rays.

She was right!

By now she was finding it difficult to think about the rays without a proper name for them. She could not simply call them "Becquerel rays" or "uranium rays." She wanted a new name, a word to make people imagine "radiating rays."

"Radioactive" was Madame Curie's word. From then on, all scientists used it, and still do.

All the samples that were not radioactive she put to one side. Now to delve deeper into the mystery of the radioactive ones. She found an interesting lump of black rock and put it between the brass plates.

The pointer jolted.

But the rock didn't have *that* much uranium or thorium. She was puzzled.

She measured other samples of the black rock. This one moved the pointer a short way, and the next . . .

Violently the pointer jumped high.

Enormously strong rays! Much stronger than uranium or thorium could give off.

Quickly she sorted out more lumps of the black, slightly shiny rock. One was four times more radioactive than other substances with the same amount of uranium. It must be a mistake!

She did the measurements again. And then again and again. Always the same answer.

Something else must be in the rock— something much more radioactive than uranium and thorium.

But she'd already tested all the elements.

The idea that entered her mind then sent a thrill right through her. A new element. An unknown substance. Something never before seen.

Her growing excitement captured Dr. Curie's attention and he took his first step onto the mountain beside her. Something was hiding in that black rock. Something was sending out extraordinary rays. Something unknown and unseen—unless they could find it.

Their search began.

This was their plan. The shiny black rock was called "pitchblende." Scientists had already worked out which of the known elements were in pitchblende. So Marie and Pierre had to separate all of these from the rock, and take them out.

Whatever was left behind must be the new element.

Their first task was to grind some pitchblende to a fine powder.

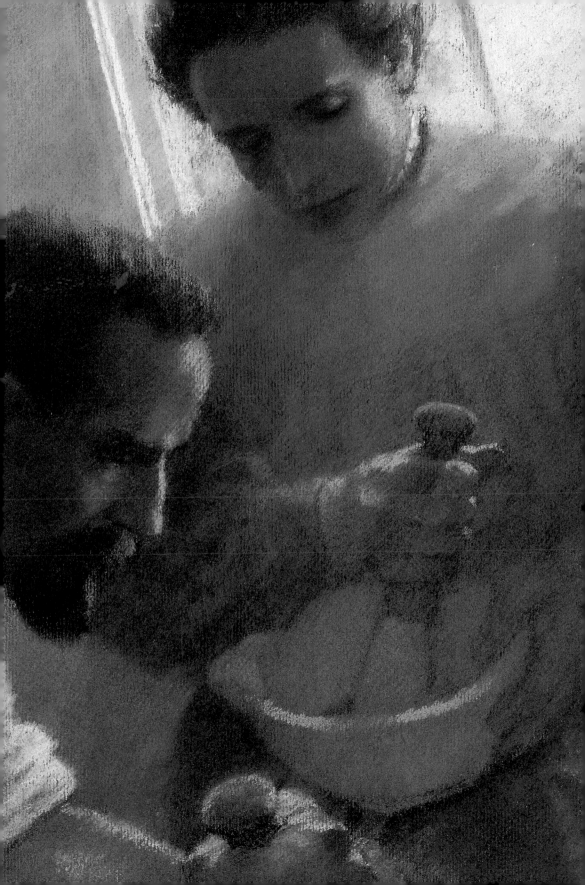

Each element needs special treatment to separate it, because each is built differently and behaves in a particular way. Some can be heated so they form a gas, like the steam in cooking. Some can be mixed with different liquids that turn the elements into hard lumps to be filtered out.

Each stage took time. Each stage needed endless care. Sometimes they made mistakes because they were tired. Sometimes they had to try several different methods before they won—heating and mixing and filtering, mixing again, heating, filtering, and so on.

But they worked on from the battle with one element to the battle with the next. And when they succeeded in removing one, Dr. Curie tested it again with his electrometer—just to be sure there were no rays. Then he tested what was left behind.

Always the pointer jolted high up the scale.

It took months to get to the hidden substance. They even chose a name for it as they worked—polonium, after Poland.

But, in 1898, when they finally got the polonium out, another puzzle faced them. Something was still left behind—and still extremely radioactive!

Another radioactive element, still hidden? Nothing else could explain the powerful rays.

But it was no use being sure it was there yet, unable to see it—even if Madame Curie did name it radium, and Dr. Curie did hope it would be beautiful. It must be in pitchblende in tiny amounts. Like one grain of sand in a bucketful! That posed a new problem. To collect enough radium to be able to see it, they needed hundreds of sacks of pitchblende—and a place big enough to hold them all.

That is how they came to the wooden shack in the schoolyard. It was leaky-roofed, earth-floored, musty, unused. But it was large, with a yard to work in so the poisonous fumes from their mixtures could float away in the open air.

Some old wooden tables; furnaces, burners, and pots to heat the substances; Dr. Curie's precious electrometer—and their laboratory was ready.

But they had no pitchblende. And no money to buy any. A new mountain of effort faced them—letter after letter was written to factory after factory. Someone, somewhere, they hoped, could spare enough pitchblende for their work.

Letter after letter came back carrying disappointment with it. A new round of letters, and then another, until—victory! A glass factory in Austria could give them tons of pitchblende waste.

One day the heavy wagon rumbled to a stop and the sacks of dark brown dirt and pine needles were piled in their yard.

The struggle to find radium in that vast heap of waste would last four long, painful years.

First they had to take a bucketful of pitchblende, and sift it to remove the pine needles and other unwanted material.

Then they ground it to a powder, put it in iron pots over a fire, and added a sodium compound.

As the mixture boiled, it separated into a small amount of radioactive solid substance and a liquid that was not radioactive.

They threw away the liquid.

They took the solid substance and dissolved it in acid.

Then began the long, slow stage of mixing this new liquid with different chemicals in turn, to make each element separate.

Bucketful after bucketful went on its journey through the sifting, mixing, heating, dissolving, filtering—sackful after sackful after sackful.

Each time they took a known element out, and Dr. Curie tested it with the electrometer.

Then he tested what was left.

The part left behind got smaller and
smaller—until it was no more than a
thimbleful that glowed in the dark.
    But its radioactivity was gigantic.
    And still they hadn't seen pure radium.
Still it hid from them.

Madame Curie lifted and carried and poured the great pots of liquid. For hours she stood over them, stirring with a gigantic iron bar.

In the summer, the shed and yard were like one enormous furnace. The heat of the coke fires and the stench of the fumes from their scientific concoctions were suffocating, almost too much to bear.

While Madame Curie stirred and mixed, Dr. Curie studied the rays from their radium-rich substance. They were so powerful and gave off such an intense heat! Vastly stronger than uranium's rays; therefore he could find out much more clearly how they behaved, what substances they could pass through, and what stopped them.

He began to realize there were at least two kinds of ray. Each behaved differently and had different strengths. And amazingly, other substances became radioactive when they were near radium.

Sometimes the Curies reeled from fatigue, working to complete a difficult task long after their brains and bodies were desperate for sleep.

Strange aches and pains flowed through them, exhausting and worrying because they seemed to have no cause. Marie's fingers were cracked and sore. And the cold in winter froze them to the bone.

Sometimes the wind gusted through gaps and cracks in the shed, and blew iron and coal dust into the little dishes cradling the radium they'd plucked from the pitchblende waste.

Then, of course, they had to start again with a new bucketful, to replace it.

And sometimes they stumbled, and months of work were lost in a pile of broken china and a glowing pool on the floor.

Three years and nine months after she first claimed that radium was in pitchblende, Marie had a tenth of a gram of her pure new element.

Enough to show the world. Victory!

Radium is over a million times more radioactive than uranium, so it was a tool of immense power. Scientists were able to use that tool to learn that radioactivity comes from *inside* the atom—the basic building block of everything in the world. And so they began to understand the atom and the gigantic energy stored inside it.

The gateway to the nuclear age stood open.

Marie Curie's tiny dish of pure radium—the labor of four long, hard years—was the beginning of a vast new story with many chapters. The story is still being written today.

When Marie Curie first found polonium and radium, she was excited because they were unknown elements. But before long she and her husband Pierre also learned that radium had important uses—it could be used to treat cancer. So Madame Curie's discovery has saved and lengthened millions of lives.

Radium also helped Marie Curie to develop some important scientific ideas. Scientists then knew that elements were made up of building blocks called atoms—but they thought that atoms were the smallest possible pieces of matter. They did not think atoms could be broken down into anything smaller. But Madame Curie wondered if radioactivity was going on inside the atoms. Perhaps there were even tinier pieces, called particles, which moved around inside the atom? Later, other scientists explored that idea, using the power of her radium. They gained new understandings of the atom, and the enormous energy that was locked inside it—nuclear energy. Our nuclear age depends on those understandings.

As years went by, scientists found many more ways of using radioactive substances. Now, radioactivity is used to run nuclear power stations and nuclear submarines; to check the thickness and quality of paper and metal in industry; to find how plants use the fertilizers they are given; to trace pollution in rivers; to test concrete under oceans; to measure the oil flow in pipelines; and to sterilize hospital equipment.

Radium made the Curies very ill. Marie Curie died from her contact with it. Now we know that radiation causes cancerous diseases, and people who work with any radioactive materials must protect themselves with clothes and equipment that keep the rays from harming them.

Marie Curie was the first woman in Europe to become a Doctor of Science. At the time, people believed that women could not understand science as well as men, nor work as hard. Madame Curie proved that she was not only as bright and hard working, she was also one of the best scientists in the world. So her story has inspired many young women, and it is now common for them to become scientists—and to be very successful at it.

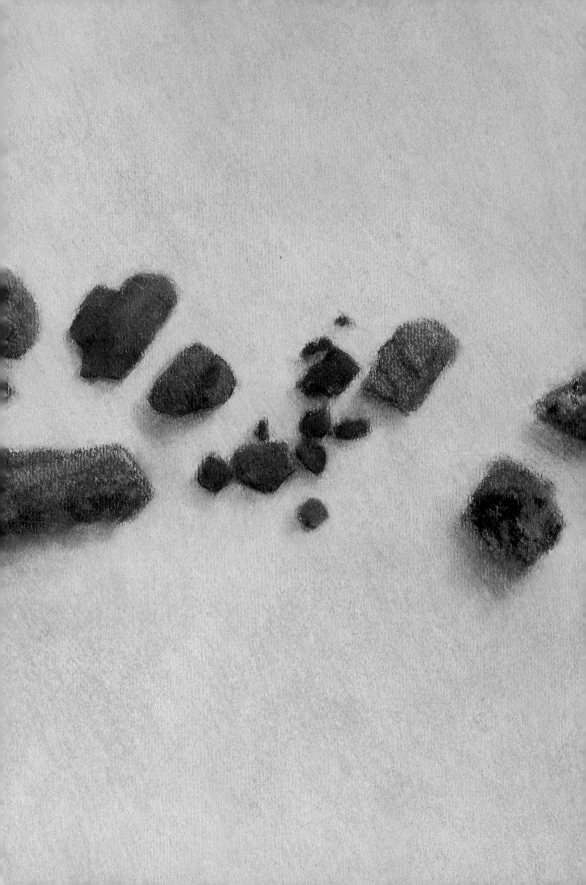

The Science Stories Books
by Beverley Birch

Benjamin Franklin's Adventures with Electricity
Illustrated by Robin Bell Corfield

Marconi's Battle for Radio
Illustrated by Robin Bell Corfield

Marie Curie's Search for Radium
Illustrated by Christian Birmingham

Pasteur's Fight against Microbes
Illustrated by Christian Birmingham